Biggest Cats in the

Billy Grinslott & Kinsey Marie Books

ISBN - 9781960612748

Caracal Cats. Their name means cat with black ears. They are often confused with lynxes. Caracals are excellent climbers. They have 20 separate muscles in their ears. They can leap 10 feet into the air. Caracals live in many areas but prefer areas that have both tree cover with open areas.

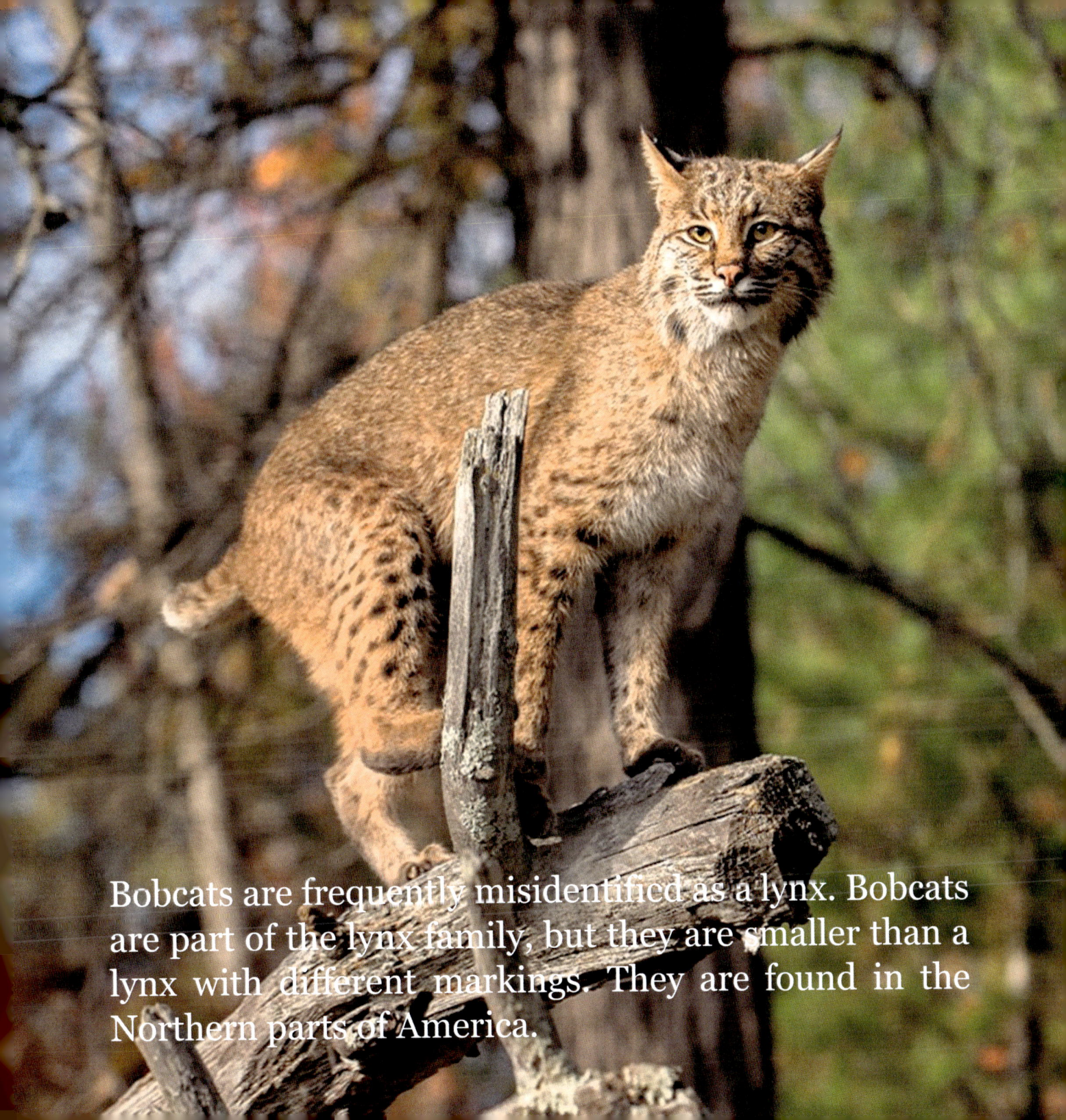

Bobcats are frequently misidentified as a lynx. Bobcats are part of the lynx family, but they are smaller than a lynx with different markings. They are found in the Northern parts of America.

The Lynx is larger than its relative the bobcat and has lighter fur and more spots than a bobcat. They are found in North America. They are mostly nocturnal cats. They like to live in dense forests. Males are slightly larger than females.

The Eurasian lynx is one of the widest ranging cats in the world and can be found in the forests of western Europe, Russia and central Asia. They are the largest of the lynx cats.

Asian golden cats are known in Thailand and Myanmar as fire cats. According to legend, carrying one hair of the Asian golden cat will protect a person from tigers. They are also known as rock cat or yellow leopard. They can grow up to 41 inches in length, and their tail can be 22 inches long. They are opportunistic feeders taking whatever food they can find.

Fishing cats are one of the few cats that are not afraid of the water. They can easily swim, and they love to catch fish. Their front toes are partially webbed, to help them when swimming. Their claws protrude slightly even when retracted. This helps them to capture fish, that are underwater.

Margays have special ankle joints that are flexible, and they can climb down trees headfirst. Margays can hang from a branch by one back foot. The Margay is most adapted cat for living in trees. They are great climbers. They are the only cat to possess the ability to rotate their hind legs 180°. Which helps to grab onto tree limbs and branches. They are native to Central and South America.

The Marbled Cat has a short, more rounded head than other felines, with a wide forehead and large pupils for seeing at night. The Marbled Cat has long enlarged upper canine teeth for grabbing onto things. They have one of the longest tails of most cats, it is very long and bushy. They use their long tail to help with their balance while climbing trees. They live mostly in southeastern Asia and the East Indies.

Sand cats have dense hair and pads on the soles of each foot that helps to protect them against the intense heat of the hot desert sand. The pads also helps them to walk across shifting and loose sand. Sand cats are fearless snake hunters. Their prey can include venomous vipers and other snakes. They are the only cat that lives primarily in the desert.

The Maine coon cat is the largest domesticated cat. A Maine Coon is in the record books as the longest domestic cat in the world, measuring over four feet long. Not to worry, these big cats are very gentle and like to be around people. They are very playful and can be walked on a leash. They also make a chirping sound, instead of a meow. They also like water and taking baths, which most cats don't.

The Andean mountain cat is a wild cat that lives in the Andes mountains. These magnificent animals are one of the rarest, and most elusive wild cats in the world. They live in rocky terrains with sparse vegetation. They also have a very long tail, that is about 70 percent of it's body length. Andean cats live a solitary life and there are very few of them. This cat is not afraid of humans.

Wildcats can live up to 15 years in captivity. Wildcats have very thick fur. They have more than 30,000 hairs per square centimeter to help keep them warm in cold climates. Wildcats have a wide range of coat colors and patterns.

Rusty spotted cats are mainly nocturnal and spend the daytime sleeping. The rusty spotted cat has a short reddish grey fur over most of its body. The rusty spotted cat is currently classified as near threatened. Not only are they incredibly fast, but rusty spotted cats can also jump up to 10 feet into the air. They are described as a smaller version of the leopard cat. The rusty spotted cat mainly lives in Asia.

African golden cats can climb, but they hunt primarily on the ground. Due to its extremely hidden living style, not much is known about this cat's behavior. African golden cats are closely related to servals and caracals. Their coat color appears in several variations, from fox-red to golden brown. The African golden cat has a compact body with shorter legs compared to its body size. African Golden cats are the only forest-dependent wild cat in Africa.

Ocelot cats. Though these cats have been spotted in states like Texas and Arkansas, they typically live in the rainforests of Central and South America. No two ocelots have the same markings on their fur. They have their own unique markings. They also have ringed bars along the full length of their tails. Ocelots are most active under the cover of darkness. The ocelot is found in South and Central America and sections of the United States.

Servals have the largest ears of any cat. Servals communicate with each other by peeing on things. Servals can purr just like house cats do. They also like to climb and sleep in trees. Servals have long, powerful legs. They have been known to jump as high as 12 feet to catch birds in mid-air.

The cougar holds the record for the animal with the highest number of names. They are the fourth largest cat in the world. The cougar has the largest range of any wild cat in the North America. A cougar can jump upward 18 feet from a sitting position. They can leap up to 30 feet horizontally. Cougars cannot roar like a lion, but they can make calls like a human scream.

The mountain lion is one of the biggest cats in North America. The largest mountain lion ever recorded weighed 276 pounds. Mountain lions don't roar like other big cats they communicate in different ways, such as chirping, growling, shrieking, and even purring.

Pumas can run as fast as 35 miles per hour. Pumas are very good climbers and know how to swim. Pumas are incredibly strong and fast predators with long bodies and powerful short legs. The hindlimbs are larger and stronger than the forelimbs, enabling them to be great leapers.

Panther is a term that refers to several species of big cats. These include leopards, jaguars, and cougars. As apex predators, panthers are essential to the habitats they live in. Their decline or removal from an area has devastating consequences. There is a panther refuge in Florida of the United States.

Black panthers can weigh up to 300 pounds. Black panthers are extremely territorial. They can run fast and climb trees with ease. They have an incredible sense of smell and incredible eyesight. They can also swim. They are members of the Jaguar or a Leopard family. They are nocturnal and their black color helps hide them at night.

Jaguars are the third largest cat in the world. Known for its jump, the word jaguar means, he who kills with one leap. They can run at speeds of up to 50 mph over short distances. They are the second fastest big cat in the world. Jaguars have the strongest bite of all cats. They also roar like other big cats. They also like to swim. Jaguars are active during both day and night. Jaguars live primarily in the rainforest.

Leopards are sometimes confused with cheetahs because of their markings. The cheetah has black spots. The leopard has round markings called rosettes. Leopards are some of the strongest cats on earth. They can climb trees even while carrying another animal. They are very elusive and good at hiding. They can run up to 35 miles per hour. They can jump 20 feet in one bounce and jump 10 feet high. That's amazing.

Snow leopards live in high-altitude mountainous areas. Snow leopards have thick fur that keeps them well insulated in cold weather. Snow leopards can't roar. They have a call described as a piercing yowl. It's so loud it can be heard for great distances. Despite being called the snow leopard, this big cat is more closely related to the tiger than the leopard. The wide, fur-covered paws of a snow leopard serve as natural snowshoes, helping to distribute its weight over soft snow and protect it from the cold.

Clouded leopards purr like small cats, but they cannot roar like other large cats. They have flexible ankle joints that allow their hind feet to rotate. They like to live in trees and can leap 15 feet from branch to branch. A Clouded Leopard can run at speeds of up to 40 miles per hour. Clouded leopards can open their mouths to an impressive 100-degree angle to grab things.

Cheetahs are the fastest cats on the planet. They can run up to 60 miles per hour in just 3 seconds. That's fast. Cheetahs are built for speed. They have a flexible spine that allows them to stretch out on each stride. Cheetahs have black spots on their fur. Cheetahs don't roar like other big cats, they meow and purr like house cats. They also have the best eyesight of any cat.

Tigers are considered one of the most beautiful cats by many, because of their astonishing looks and black stripes. Tigers are the largest amongst all the wild cats. They are strong and can knock things down with one swipe of their paw. Tiger cubs are born blind until their eyes develop. Tigers live for 25 years, and they love to swim and play in the water.

We saved this cat for last. Do you know what it is? It is a male lion. Male lions are known as the king of the jungle because of their raw power and strength. Lions don't fear other animals. The roar of a male lion can be heard 5 miles away. Lions like to live in groups known as a pride. Male lions have mains and females do not. Female lions gather most of the food and male lions protect the herd and the young cubs, baby lions.

Author Page

Billy Grinslott & Kinsey Marie Books

Copyright, All Rights Reserved

ISBN - 9781960612748

Made in the USA
Middletown, DE
17 March 2024